gertrude
stein's
america

"America dear America the United States of America."..

gertrude stein's america

edited by Gilbert A. Harrison

ROBERT B. LUCE, INC.

Washington, D.C.

Grateful acknowledgment is made to the following for permission to include the copyrighted selections included in this work:

The Autobiography of Alice B. Toklas,
    © 1933 by Harcourt Brace and Company, Inc.
    Reprinted by permission of Random House, Inc.
Everybody's Autobiography, © 1937 by Random House, Inc.
Wars I Have Seen, © 1945 by Random House, Inc.
Brewsie and Willie, © 1946 by Random House, Inc.
Lectures in America, © 1935 by The Modern Library, Inc.
    All the above reprinted by permission of Random House, Inc.
"A Patriotic Leading" from *Useful Knowledge,* published by The
    Bodley Head Limited, John Lane London, 1928
    Reprinted by permission of Harcourt Brace and World, Inc.
Four in America, © 1947 by Alice B. Toklas
    Reprinted by permission of the Yale University Press
Narration, © 1935 by the University of Chicago
    Reprinted by permission of The University of Chicago Press
Picasso, published by B. T. Batsford London, 1938
    Reprinted by permission of the estate of Gertrude Stein
Paris France, published by B. T. Batsford London, 1940
    Reprinted by permission of the estate of Gertrude Stein
What Are Masterpieces, © 1940 by Gertrude Stein
    Reprinted by permission of Conference Press
"Off We All Went to See Germany," © 1945 Time Inc.
    Reprinted courtesy *Life*
"The New Hope in Our 'Sad Young Men,' " © 1945 by The New
    York Times Company
    Reprinted by permission
"How Writing is Written," © 1935 by the Choate Literary Magazine
    Reprinted by permission of the Choate Literary Magazine
"American Food and American Houses"
"American Cities and How They Differ from Each Other"
    Interview, "Gertrude Stein Adores U.S. but Not California,"
    © 1935 The New York Herald Tribune
    Reprinted by permission of The New York Herald Tribune
Article which appeared in the continental edition of Yank, The
    Army Weekly, November 11, 1945, reprinted by permission of
    the Department of Defense.

...A patriotic leading

Indeed indeed.   Verse *I*
Can you see.
The stars.
And regularly the precious treasure.
What do we love without measure.
We know.

We suspect the second man.   Verse *II*

We are worthy of everything that happens.   Verse *III*
You mean weddings.
Naturally I mean weddings.

And then we are.   Verse *IV*
Hail to the nation.

Do you think we believe it.   Verse *V*

It is that or bust.   Verse *VI*

Contents

Introduction   9

The Doughboys   19

The GI's   29

Landscape   45

We and They   63

Success   75

Language   89

Notes on Sources   101

Introduction

Gertrude Stein said she "always remained firmly born in Allegheny, Pennsylvania." It was a trial to French officials in the first World War who tried to spell it. She left Allegheny when she was six months old; grew up in Oakland, California; in 1892, when she was eighteen, moved to Baltimore, where she remained briefly; and in 1903 settled in France. She returned to the United States only once, yet she never lost her ardor for America, her American manner and accent.

With the exception of the earliest stories—Things As They Are and Three Lives—and the autobiographical narratives—The Autobiography of Alice B. Toklas, Everybody's Autobiography, and Wars I Have Seen, her work had and has a small audience; a large part of it was not published during her lifetime. Her dominating literary interest was in the "exact description of inner and outer reality," yet her plays and portraits, her studies of creativity and her teasing experiments with words convey little reality to most readers.

But if what she wrote did not get across easily, she did. In the 1920's and 30's, scores of talented young Americans came to her home in Paris at 27 rue de

Fleurus (Hemingway, Fitzgerald, Wilder, Carl Van Vechten, Sherwood Anderson, Elliot Paul, Louis Bromfield, Robert Coates, Virgil Thomson, Henry McBride), listened attentively and came back for more, because she compelled attention. She understood them and their problems. She spoke to their point. And some of them, when they became famous, did not forgive her astuteness. But they never forgot her, or the liberating quality of her mind. Carl Van Vechten quotes a student as saying, when she visited Amherst College in 1934: "I was dead against her and I just went to see what she looked like and then she took the door of my mind right off its hinges and now it's wide open." Perhaps William James had done that for her when she was his student in the early '90's. At any rate, we know that after Miss Stein had gone to Paris and begun to buy pictures by Matisse, Picasso and Juan Gris, Professor James came to see her and her paintings. They were not for him; he could only tell her, as he had at Radcliffe, that he always believed in keeping an open mind.

Gertrude Stein came of a well-to-do, middle-class family, and for her the middle class always remained "the very best the world can ever know." In Things As They Are, Helen asks her friend to explain what she means by calling herself middle class: "From the little I have seen of you I think that you are quite right when you say that you are reasonable and just but surely to understand others and even to understand oneself is the last thing a middle class person cares to do." Adele (Miss

Stein) replies: "I never claimed to be middle class in my intellect and in truth, I probably have the experience of all apostles, I am rejected by the class whose cause I preach but that has nothing to do with the case. I simply contend that the middle class ideal which demands that people be affectionate, respectable, honest and content, that they avoid excitements and cultivate serenity is the ideal that appeals to me, it is in short the ideal of affectionate family life, of honorable business methods."

In 1875, when Gertrude Stein was a year old, her family took her to Europe where they spent four years, most of it in Austria. They then moved to California, and here Gertrude Stein experienced her "first conscious esthetic pleasure . . . a sunset in East Oakland, the sun setting in a cavern of cloud." In 1893 she enrolled at what was then called Harvard Annex, where she studied biology, psychology, philosophy and history. On the advice of Professor James, she entered Johns Hopkins Medical School, but by the time of final exams she had decided that medicine bored her. She blithely dismissed the medical degree that was just within reach, left America and went to Paris to join her brother Leo. "Paris was the place," she said, "that suited us who were to create the twentieth century art and literature." Apart from occasional trips to Spain, Italy and England, and a triumphant lecture tour in her own country in 1934-5, she stayed in France until her death in Paris in 1946.

"It has always seemed to me a rare privilege, this, of

being an American," she wrote in The Making of Americans, that epic, imaginative history of a "decent family's progress"—"a real American, one whose tradition it has taken scarcely sixty years to create. We need only realize our parents, remember our grandparents and know ourselves and our history is complete. The old people in a new world, the new people made out of the old, that is the story that I mean to tell . . ."

One could not think of Miss Stein or of her companion, Alice B. Toklas, as expatriates. But why, sentimental as they were about America, did they choose to live abroad? Miss Stein thought about that question. She concluded that "everybody who writes is interested in living inside themselves in order to tell what is inside themselves. That is why writers have to have two countries, the one where they belong and the one in which they live really. The second one is romantic, it is separate from themselves, it is not real but it is really there."

There were other reasons, money for one. Gertrude Stein earned almost nothing until she wrote the Autobiography of Alice B. Toklas, and not much after that. It was easier in Paris, easier than in America in the years from before World War I to the beginning of World War II, to live in her elegantly simple manner on the modest income provided by an older brother.

But there is another explanation for a residence abroad that was never a rejection of her native land. She expressed it in the most personal way in The Making of Americans, when she said that "singularity that is neither crazy, sporty, faddish, or a fashion, or low class distinction, such a singularity, I say, we have not made enough of yet so that any other one can really know it, it is as yet an unknown product with us. It takes time to make queer people, and have others who can know it, time and a certainty of place and means. Custom, fashions, and a feel for Mother Earth are needed to breed vital singularity in any man and alas how poor we are in all these three. Brother Singulars, we are misplaced in a generation that knows not Joseph. We feel before the disapproval of our cousins, the courageous condescension of our friends who gallantly sometimes agree to walk the streets with us, from all of them who never anyway can understand why such ways and not the others are so dear to us, we fly to the kindly comforts of an older world accustomed to take all manner of strange forms into its bosom . . ."

She liked France too because there she was surrounded by "people who don't know english." It left her "more intensely alone with my eyes and my english. I do not know if it would have been possible to have english be so all and all to me otherwise. And they none of them could read a word I wrote, most of them did not even know that I did write. No, I like living with so very many people and being all alone with english and myself."

She was interested in the essence of a person or place, in how different nations cooked, counted, what they ate, and why. She noted how distinctly the soldiers of different countries marched in the first World War. In the second war, having chosen to remain in the French countryside in the Rhone valley, she listened to the radio and wrote about the variety of national broadcasts: "The English always begin with Here is London, or the BBC home service, or the overseas service, always part of a pleasant home life, of supreme importance to any English man or any English woman. The Americans say with poetry and fire, This is the Voice of America, and then with modesty and good neighborliness, one of the United Nations, it is the voice of America speaking to you across the Atlantic. Then the Frenchmen say, Frenchmen speaking to Frenchmen, and they always begin like that, and the Belgiums are simple and direct, they just announce radio Belge, and the national anthem, and the French also say, honor and country, and the Swiss so politely say, the studio of Geneva . . . and Italy says, live Mussolini, live Italy, and they make a bird noise and then they start, and Germany starts like this, Germany calling, Germany calling. In the last war I said that the camouflage was the distinctive characteristic of each country, each nation stamped itself upon its camouflage, but in this war it is the heading of the broadcast that makes national life so complete and determined. It is that a nation is even stronger than the personality of anyone, it certainly is so nations must go on, they certainly must."

Individuals, families, nations in their uniqueness and sameness absorbed her, and so did ideas in so far as they accurately expressed "things as they are." The other kind of ideas were those held by what she called intellectual people, of whom she had "a horror." She questioned closely and listened to the answers. She spoke firmly, often beginning with the command: "Now look!" In another, the manner would have been arrogant. In her it seemed plain and sensible. But talking for her was not creation. "Remarks," she told Hemingway, "are not literature," nor is recollection, however interesting. She once described talking with several American reporters and a photographer. "You know it's funny," she told them, "that the photographer is the one of the lot of you who looks as if he were intelligent and who is listening now why is that, you do I said to the photographer you do understand what I'm talking about, don't you. 'Of course I do,' he said, 'you see I can listen to what you say because I don't have to remember what you are saying, they can't listen because they've got to remember.'" And Miss Stein added, "I found that very interesting and of course it is so, of course nobody can listen if they have to remember what they are hearing. That is the trouble with newspapers and teaching with government and history."

Miss Stein was a self-starter, self-made. Her dress, her thoughts, her work were original, and she looked for that in others. It didn't matter what any writer chose as his subject; it was his individual way of seeing things that concerned her; she never criticized any detail of anyone's writing.

But it is Gertrude Stein as an American that gives this book its theme. It is not true, as she thought, that "one is always proud of the places your people come from," but it was true for her. She wrote, in Things As They Are, of Adele going to Boston and steeping herself "in the very essence of clear-eyed Americanism. For days she wandered about the Boston streets rejoicing in the passionless intelligence of the faces. She revelled in the American streetcar crowd with its ready intercourse, free comments and airy persiflage all without double meanings which created an atmosphere that never suggested for a moment the need to be on guard. It was a cleanliness that began far inside of these people and was kept persistently washed by a constant current of clean cold water." The time was the turn of the century, and today that may not be "the very essence of clear-eyed Americanism." But it remained so to her. "You're the flagpole on which it all stands," her friend Sylvia Beach told her after they had come to know each other in Paris. She said of herself that "she was not efficient, she was good humored, she was democratic, one person was as good as another, and she knew what she wanted done." And she added that "if you are like that . . . anybody will do anything for you. The important thing . . . is that you must have deep down as the deepest thing in you a sense of equality."

Her confidence in the everlasting self-reliance of Americans weakened during the '30's, and the worry that began then deepened as she met G.I.'s in the second

16

World War. It was not that America would become poor, but that perhaps it had become "too old to become young again," that employees were "getting to feel themselves employed and not potential employers."

Here are gathered some of Gertrude Stein's observations on her country drawn from her autobiographies, essays, novels, plays, poems and lectures. Selections from the Autobiography of Alice B. Toklas are of course in the third person, since Miss Stein chose to write her own story in another's name, "as Defoe did the autobiography of Robinson Crusoe." All source references are in the appendix.

My thanks go to the publishers of Gertrude Stein's work, especially Bennett Cerf of Random House, for allowing the reprinting here of material under their copyright.

GILBERT A. HARRISON

WASHINGTON, D. C., 1965

SOLDIERS: *the doughboys*

. . . .

"There is something in this native land business
and you cannot get away from it,
in peace time you do not seem to notice it much
particularly when you live in foreign parts
but when there is a war and you are all alone
and completely cut off from knowing about your country
well then there it is,
your native land is your native land,
it certainly is."

"Auntie," the Ford car Gertrude Stein drove in World War I for the American Fund for French Wounded, arrived in early 1917 and until the Armistice Miss Stein and Miss Toklas were perfectly ready to "crank the car as often as there was nobody else to do it." There usually was somebody else. To one soldier who had been helpful, Miss Stein said, "but you are tellement, gentil, very nice and kind." "Madame," said he quite simply, "all soldiers are nice and kind." They were to her.

In Nevers, they met the doughboys: "There we first heard what Gertrude Stein calls the sad song of the marines, which tells how everybody else in the american army has at some time mutinied, but the marines never." They spent an evening at the YMCA in Nevers and "saw for the first time in many years americans just americans, the kind that would not naturally ever have come to Europe." Miss Stein wanted to know "what state and what city they came from, what they did, how old they were and how they liked it." One of those soldiers described her "sandals buckled on over the ankles, a full skirt, knitted vest and shirtwaist with sleeves gathered at the wrists . . . homely with no elegance at all, and still somehow regal."

"Auntie" survived the war and was driven back to Paris, where Miss Stein and Miss Toklas watched the allies march under the Arc de Triomphe. They had to admit the French carried their flags best of all, but still "Pershing and his officer carrying the flag behind him were perhaps the most perfectly spaced."

☆ ☆ ☆

I was young then but I can still see those young men in San Francisco, those middle-western young men of twenty and twenty-one, with their undeveloped necks, their rather doughy faces, I see why they call them dough-boys, they are like that between twenty and twenty-one, they go to sleep anywhere sitting or standing . . .

☆ ☆ ☆

Soon the american army came to Nîmes. One day Madame Fabre met us and said that her cook had seen some american soldiers. She must have mistaken some english soldiers for them, we said. Not at all, she answered, she is very patriotic. At any rate the american soldiers came, a regiment of them of the S.O.S. the service of supply, how well I remember how they used to say it with the emphasis on the of.

We soon got to know them all well and some of them very well. There was Duncan, a southern boy with such a very marked southern accent that when he was well into a story I was lost. Gertrude Stein whose people all come from Baltimore had no difficulty and they used to shout with laughter together, and all I could understand was that they had killed him as if he was a chicken. The people in Nîmes were as much troubled as I was. A great many of the ladies in Nîmes spoke english very well. There had always been english governesses in Nîmes and they, the nimoises had always prided themselves on their knowledge of english but as they said not only could they not understand these americans but these americans could not understand them when they spoke english. I had to admit that it was more or less the same with me.

The soldiers were all Kentucky, South Carolina etcetera and they were hard to understand.

Duncan was a dear. He was supply-sergeant to the camp and when we began to find american soldiers here and there in french hospitals we always took Duncan along to give the american soldier pieces of his lost uniform and white bread. Poor Duncan was miserable because he was not at the front. He had enlisted as far back as the expedition to Mexico and here he was well in the rear and no hope of getting away because he was one of the few who understood the complicated system of army book-keeping and his officers would not recommend him for the front. I will go, he used to say bitterly, they can bust me if they like I will go. But as we told him there were plenty of A.W.O.L. absent without leave the south was full of them, we were always meeting them and they would say, say any military police around here. Duncan was not made for that life. Poor Duncan.

Two days before the armistice, he came in to see us and he was drunk and bitter. He was usually a sober boy but to go back and face his family never having been to the front was too awful. He was with us in a little sitting-room and in the front room were some of his officers and it would not do for them to see him in that state and it was time for him to get back to the camp. He had fallen half asleep with his head on the table. Duncan, said Gertrude Stein sharply, yes, he said. She said to him, listen Duncan. Miss Toklas is going to stand up, you stand up too and you fix your eyes right on the back of her head, do you understand. Yes, he said. Well then she will start to walk and you follow her and don't you for a moment move your eyes from the back of her head until you are in my car. Yes, he said. And he did and Gertrude Stein drove him to the camp.

Dear Duncan. It was he who was all excited by the news that the americans had taken forty villages at Saint-Mihiel. He was to go with us that afternoon to Avignon to deliver some cases. He was sitting very straight on the step and all of a sudden his eye was caught by some houses. What are they, he asked. Oh just a village, Gertrude Stein said. In a minute there were some more houses. And what are those houses, he asked. Oh just a village. He fell very silent and he looked at the landscape as he had never looked at it before. Suddenly with a deep sigh, forty villages ain't so much, he said.

We did enjoy the life with these doughboys, I would like to tell nothing but doughboy stories. They all got on amazingly well with the french. They worked together in the repair sheds of the railroad. The only thing that bothered the americans were the long hours. They worked too concentratedly to keep it up so long. Finally an arrangement was made that they should have their work to do in their hours and the french in theirs. There was a great deal of friendly rivalry. The american boys did not see the use of putting so much finish on work that was to be shot up so soon again, the french said that they could not complete work without finish. But both lots thoroughly liked each other.

Gertrude Stein always said the war was so much better than just going to America. Here you were with America in a kind of way that if you only went to America you could not possibly be. Every now and then one of the american soldiers would get into the hospital at Nîmes and as Doctor Fabre knew that Gertrude Stein had had a medical education he always wanted her present with the doughboy on these occasions. One of them fell off the train. He did not believe that the little french trains could go fast but they did, fast enough to kill him.

This was a tremendous occasion. Gertrude Stein in company with the wife of the préfet, the governmental head of the department and the wife of the general were the chief mourners. Duncan and two others blew on the bugle and everybody made speeches. The Protestant pastor asked Gertrude Stein about the dead man and his virtues and she asked the doughboys. It was difficult to find any virtue. Apparently he had been a fairly hard citizen. But can't you tell me something good about him she said despairingly. Finally Taylor, one of his friends, looked up solemnly and said, I tell you he had a heart as big as a washtub.

☆☆☆

. . . after about forty kilometres, we saw on the road some american ambulance men. Where can we get our car fixed. Just a little farther, they said. We went a little farther and there found an american ambulance outfit. They had no extra mud-guard but they could give us a new triangle. I told our troubles to the sergeant, he grunted and said a word in an undertone to a mechanic. Then turning to us he said gruffly, run-her-in. Then the mechanic took off his tunic and threw it over the radiator. As Gertrude Stein said when any american did that the car was his.

☆☆☆

The next day she spent with California and Iowa in the garage, as she called the two soldiers who were detailed to fix up her car. She was pleased with them when every time there was a terrific noise anywhere, they said solemnly to each other, that french chauffeur is just changing gears. Gertrude Stein, Iowa and California enjoyed themselves so thoroughly that I am sorry to say the car did not last out very well after we left Nevers, but at any rate we did get to Paris.

☆ ☆ ☆

The Trail of the Lonesome Pine as a song made a lasting appeal to Gertrude Stein. Mildred Aldrich had it among her records and when we spent the afternoon with her at Huiry, Gertrude Stein inevitably would start The Trail of the Lonesome Pine on the phonograph and play it and play it. She liked it in itself and she had been fascinated during the war with the magic of The Trail of the Lonesome Pine as a book for the doughboy. How often when a doughboy in hospital had become particularly fond of her, he would say, I once read a great book, do you know it, it is called the Trail of the Lonesome Pine. They finally got a copy of it in the camp at Nîmes and it stayed by the bedside of every sick soldier. They did not read much of it, as far as she could make out sometimes only a paragraph, in the course of several days, but their voices were husky when they spoke of it, and when they were particularly devoted to her they would offer to lend her this very dirty and tattered copy.

She reads anything and naturally she read this and she was puzzled. It had practically no story to it and it was not exciting, or adventurous, and it was very well written and was mostly description of mountain scenery. Later on she came across some reminiscences of a southern woman who told how the mountaineers in the southern army during the civil war used to wait in turn to read Victor Hugo's Les Misérables, an equally astonishing thing for again there is not much of a story and a great deal of description. However, Gertrude Stein admits that she loves the song of The Trail of the Lonesome Pine in the same way that the doughboy loved the book . . .

SOLDIERS: *the GI's*

. . . .

"*It is pretty wonderful and pretty awful
to have been intimate and friendly and proud
of two American armies in France
apart only by twenty-seven years. It is wonderful
and if I could live twenty-seven more years
could I see them here again.
No I do not think so,
maybe in other places but not here.
In the beginning when the Americans were here
we had officers and their companion drivers.
They were companion drivers, companions and drivers
drivers and companions.
The French revolution said, liberty brotherhood
and equality,
well they said it and we are it, bless us.*"

"Nothing ever does get settled," Miss Stein knew. Yet she had been "terribly sure" that there would be no second World War. When it came, she made "quite a scene." But there it was, so it had to be won. She was living at the time in a rented house in the countryside near Belley, not far from Switzerland. In 1943 she moved further up the Rhone, to Culoz. It would have been prudent to leave France after the capitulation of Petain. She could have gone to Spain or returned to the United States. She was not only an American but a Jewess. There were Germans nearby. She made little effort to be inconspicuous. "They're always trying to get us to leave France," she wrote, "but here we are and here we stay." The days were spent walking about the countryside, collecting food and rumors, waiting. At last the Americans, the Americans who "do everything for you," came, and Miss Stein fell in love with her second generation of American soldiers.

☆ ☆ ☆

It is very tantalising Americans all over the place sometimes only twenty kilometers away and we do not see them, how we want to see them and send word to America and have news from them. To-night I was all bitten by mosquitoes trying to get more news of them. I went down to the Pont de la Lois which is the only bridge left over the Rhone, it strangely enough was not destroyed in '40 and now again it has not been destroyed. It was near there that our little battle was fought and it was near there that the bomb were dropped the other day or was it only yesterday. Well anyway I was talking to the maquis that were guarding the bridge, among them a boy I knew in Cezerieu and they told me that a car with American officers had passed over the bridge, when I told Alice Toklas about it tonight she said she would take her typewriting down there and await them but when I told her about mosquitoes she weakened, well anyway, one of the train hands who was also there said that they had received orders to repair the train tracks between Chambrey and Culoz and that it had to be done in three days, because he said the Americans want to use it and he promised me that when the first train carrying Americans was signaled, night or day, he would leave all and come up and let me know. Dear Americans how we do want to see them.

This is the way it happened. We go to Belley about once a month to go shopping and the bank and things like that and yesterday Thursday was the day, so we went over in a taxi, and when we got to Belley as I got out of the taxi several people said to me, Americans are here. I had heard that so often that I had pretty well given up hope and I said oh nonesense but yes they said, and then the son of the watchmaker who had been the most stead-fast and violent pro-ally even in the darkest days came up to me and said the Americans are here. Really I said yes he said well I said lead me to them, all right he said they are at the hotel so we went on just as fast as we could and when we got to the hotel they tried to stop me but we said no and went in. I saw the proprietor of the hotel and I said is it true there are Americans, yes he said come on, and I followed and there we were Alice Toklas panting behind and Basket very excited and we went into a room filled with maquis and the mayor of Belley and I said in a loud voice are there any Americans here and three men stood up and they were Americans God bless them and were we pleased. We held each other's hands and we patted each other and we sat down together and I told them who we were, and they knew, I always take it for granted that people will know who I am and at the same time at the last moment I kind of doubt, but they knew of course they knew, they were Lieutenant Walter E. Oleson 120th Engineers and

Private Edward Landry and Walter Hartze, and they belonged to the Thunderbirds and how we talked and how we patted each other in the good American way, and I had to know where they came from and where they were going and where they were born. In the last war we had come across our first American soldiers and it had been nice but nothing like this, after almost two years of not a word with America, there they were, all three of them. Then we went to look at their car the jeep, and I had expected it to be much smaller but it was quite big and they said did I want a ride and I said you bet I wanted a ride and we all climbed in and there I was riding in an American army car driven by an American soldier. Everybody was so excited.

Then we all said good-bye and we did hope to see them again, and then we went on with our shopping, then suddenly everybody got excited army trucks filled with soldiers were coming along but not Americans, this was the French army in American cars and they were happy and we were happy and tired and happy and then we saw two who looked like Americans in a car standing alone and I went over and said are you Americans and they said sure, and by that time I was confident and I said I was Gertrude Stein and did they want to come back with us and spend the night. They said well yes they thought that the war could get along without them for a few hours so they came, Alice Toklas got into the car with the driver and the colonel came with me, oh a joyous moment and we all drove home and the village was wild with excitement and they all wanted to shake the colonel's hand and last we got into the house, and were we excited. Here was the first Americans actually in the house with us, impossible to believe that only three weeks before the Germans had been in the village still and feeling themselves masters, it was wonderful. Lieutenant Colonel William O. Perry Headquarters 47th Infantry Division and private John Schmaltz, wonderful that is all I can say about it wonderful, and I said you are going to sleep in beds where German officers slept six weeks ago, wonderful my gracious perfectly wonderful.

How we talked that night, they just brought all America to us every bit of it, they came from Colorado, lovely Colorado, I do not know Colorado but that is the way I felt about it lovely Colorado and then everybody was tired out and they gave us nice American specialties and my were we happy, we were, completely and truly happy and completely and entirely worn out with emotion. The next morning while they breakfasted we talked some more and we patted each other and then kissed each other and then they went away. Just as we were sitting down to lunch, in came four more Americans this time war correspondents, our emotions were not yet exhausted nor our capacity to talk, how we talked and talked where they were born was music to the ears Baltimore and Washington, D.C. and Detroit and Chicago, it is all music to the ears so long long long away from the names of the places where they were born. Well they have asked me to go with them to Voiron to broadcast with them to America next Sunday and I am going and the war is over and this certainly this is the last war to remember.

☆ ☆ ☆

. . . yes they were American boys but they had a poise and completely lacked the provincialism which did characterise the last American army, they talked and they listened and they had a sureness, they were quite certain of themselves, they had no doubts or uncertainties and they had not to make any explanations. The last army was rather given to explaining, oh just anything, they were given to explaining, these did not explain, they were just conversational.

Then more troop trains came along and we took apples down to them and we talked to them and they talked to us and I was getting more impressed with their being different, they knew where they were and what they were and why they were, yes they did, they had poise and not any of them was ever drunk, not a bit, it was most exciting that they were like that.

The last American army used to ask questions, why do the French people put walls around their houses what are they afraid of what do they want to hide. Why do they want to stay and work this ground when there is so much better land to find. This army does not ask questions like that, they consider that people have their habits and their ways of living, some you can get along with and others you can't, but they all are perfectly reasonable for the people who use them. That is the great change in the Americans, they are interested, they are observant, they are accustomed to various types of people and ways of being, they have plenty of curiosity, but not any criticism, that is the new army. It was all very exciting.

Then one day down at the station, it was raining, I saw three American soldiers standing, I said hello what are you doing, why we just came here, they said, to stay a few days. I laughed. Is it A.W.O.L. I said or do you call it something else now, well no they said we still call it that. And said I what are you going to do, just stay a few days they said. Come along I said, even if you are A.W.O.L. you will have to be given some tea and cake so come along. They came. One from Detroit, one little one from Tennessee, one big one from New Jersey. We talked, it seemed somehow more like that old army, their being A.W.O.L. and deciding to stay here a few days. They came back with me, and we talked. They were interested, Tennessee said honestly he was tired of ten inch shells, he just had had enough of ten inch shells. The other two seemed to be just tired, they were not particular what they were tired of, they were just tired. We talked and then in talking to them I began to realise that men from the South seemed to be quite often men who had been orphans since they were children, the men from Tennessee and from Arkansas seemed to tend to be orphans from very young, they were members of large families and the large family once having been made, they promptly became orphans, I also began to realise that there were lots of pure American families where there were lots of brothers and sisters. The last army seven to eleven in a family was rare, but now it seemed to be quite common. Not emigrant families but pure American families. I was very much interested. And now the difference between the old army and the new began to be so real to me that I began to ask the American army about it. In the meanwhile the three A.W.O.L.s after moving into the village and then moving out and then moving in again did finally move out. They came to see us before they left, they did not say where they were going and they said it had been a pleasure to know us.

In the meanwhile, five M.P.s had come to stay in the station to watch the stuff on the trains and see that it did not get stolen, and with these we got to be very good friends, and they were the first ones with whom I began to talk about the difference between the last army and this army. Why is it, I said.

They said, yes we know we are different, and I said and how did you find it out. From what we heard about the other army, that made us know we were very different, I said there is no doubt about that, you don't drink much

I said, no we don't and we save our money they said, we don't want to go home and when we get there not have any money, we want to have a thousand dollars or so at least to be able to look around and to find out what we really want to do. (Even the three A.W.O.L.s felt like that about money.) Well I explained what one used to complain of about American men was that as they grew older they did not grow more interesting, they grew duller. When I made that lecture tour in '35 to the American universities I used to say to them, now all sorts of things interest you but what will happen to you five years hence when you are working at some job will things interest you or will you just get dull. Yes said one of the soldiers yes but you see the depression made them know that a job was not all there was to it as mostly there was no job, and if there was it was any kind of job not the kind of job they had expected it to be, you would see a college man digging on the road doing anything and so we all came to find out you might just as well be interested in anything since anyway your job might not be a job and if it was well then it was not the kind of job it might have been. Yes that did a lot, they all said, it certainly did do a lot.

Yes said one of the younger ones even if you were only kids during the depression you got to feel that way about it. Anyway they all agreed the depression had a lot to do with it.

There is one thing in which this army is not different from that other army that is in being generous and sweet and particularly kind to children.

They are sweet and kind and considerate all of them, how they do think about what you need and what will please you, they did then that other army and they do now this army.

When our M.P.s had got settled completely in their box car I used to go down to see them, and one day one of the mothers in the town told me that her nine year old daughter had been praying every single day that she might see an American soldier and she never had and now the mother was beginning to be afraid that the child would lose faith in prayer. I said I would take her down to see the American soldiers and we went. Naturally they were sweet and each one of them thought of something to give her, candies chewing gum, one of them gave her one of the U.S. badges they wear on their caps and one gave her a medal that the Pope had blessed in Rome and given to the American soldiers. And she was so happy, she sang them all the old French songs, Claire de la Lune, The Good King Dagobert and On the Bridge of Avignon.

Then as we were going home I said to her, about that chewing gum you must chew it but be careful not to swallow it. Oh yes I know she said. How do you know that I asked oh she said because when there was the last war my mother was a little girl and the American soldiers gave her chewing gum and all through this war my mother used to tell us about it, and she gave a rapturous sigh and said and now I have it.

☆ ☆ ☆

It was late afternoon and the streets were narrow and three Negro soldiers came along, there was a very little girl and her mother, one of the Negroes fell on his knee like a cavalier before the little girl and took her hand, the mother went on and then stood slightly flushed looking at her little girl, the little girl a little flushed shook the hand of the kneeling soldier, he said a word in French, she answered him, she was a very little girl, only five years old, the other two had gone on, he rose from his knee and he went on, the little girl went along with her mother.

☆ ☆ ☆

Gradually as the joy and excitement of really having Americans here really have them here began to settle a little I began to realise that Americans converse much more than they did, American men in those other days, the days before these days did not converse. How well I remember in the last war seeing four or five of them at a table at a hotel and one man would sort of drone along monologuing about what he had or had not done and the others solemnly and quietly eating and drinking and never saying a word. And seeing the soldiers stand at a corner or be seated somewhere and there they were and minutes hours passed and they never said a word, and then one would get up and leave and the others got up and left and that was that. No this army was not like that, this army conversed, it talked it listened, and each one of them had something to say no this army was not like that other army. People do not change, no they don't, when I was in America after almost thirty years of absence they asked me if I did not find Americans changed and I said no what could they change to except to be Americans and anyway I could have gone to school with any of them they were just like the ones I went to school with and now they are still Americans but they can converse and they are interesting when they talk. The older Americans always told stories that was about all there was to their talking but these don't tell stories they converse and what they say is interesting and what they hear interests them and that does make them different not really different God bless them but just the same they are not quite the same.

We did not talk about that then. We had too much to tell and they had too much to tell to spend any time conversing about conversation. What we always wanted to know was the state they came from and what they did before they came over here. One said that he was born on a race track and worked in a night club. Another was the golf champion of Mississippi, but what we wanted most was to hear them say the name of the state in which they were born and the names of the other states where they had lived.

After every war, there have only been two like that but I do not think that just to say after the other war makes it feel as it does, no I do mean after every war, it feels like that, after every war when I talk and listen to all our army, it feels like that too, the thing I like most are the names of all the states of the United States. They make music and they are poetry, you do not have to recite them all but you just say any one two three four or five of them and you will see they make music and they make poetry.

☆ ☆ ☆

That evening I went over to talk to the soldiers, and to hear what they had to say, we all got very excited, Sergeant Santiani who had asked me to come complained that I confused the minds of his men but why shouldn't their minds be confused, gracious goodness, are we going to be like the Germans, only believe in the Aryans that is our own race, a mixed race if you like but all having the same point of view. I got very angry with them, they admitted they like the Germans better than the other Europeans. Of course you do, I said, they flatter you and they obey you, when the other countries don't like you and say so and personally you have not been awfully ready to meet them half way, well naturally if they don't like you they show it, the Germans don't like you but they flatter you, doggone it, I said I bet you Fourth of July they will all be putting up our flag and all you big babies will just be flattered to death, literally to death, I said bitterly, because you will have to fight again. Well said one of them after all we are on top. Yes I said and is there any spot on earth more dangerous than on top. You don't like the Latins, or the Arabs or the Wops, or the British, well don't you forget a country can't live without friends, I want you all to get to understand other countries so that you can be friends, make a little effort, try to find out what it is all about. We got very excited, they passed me cognac, but I don't drink so they found me some grapefruit juice, and they patted me and sat me down, and there it all was.

LANDSCAPE

. . . .

"After all anybody is as their land and air is.
Anybody is as the sky is low or high,
the air heavy or clear
and anybody is as there is wind or no wind there.
It is that which makes them and the arts they make
and the work they do and the way they eat
and the way they drink
and the way they learn and everything."

"There is no passion more dominant and instinctive in the human spirit," Miss Stein wrote in Things As They Are, "than the need of the country to which one belongs. One often speaks of homesickness as if in its intense form it were the peculiar property of Swiss mountaineers, Scandinavians, Frenchmen and those other nations that too have a poetic background, but poetry is no element in the case. It is simply a vital need for the particular air that is native, whether it is the used up atmosphere of London, the clean-cut cold of America or the rarified air of Swiss mountains. The time comes when nothing in the world is so important as a breath of ones own particular climate. If it were ones last penny it would be used for that return passage."

In the autumn of 1934, after thirty-one years abroad, Miss Stein returned to the United States to lecture. She stayed less than six months, travelling across the country from New England, through the South to "hot and delicious" New Orleans, and on to the Southwest and the Pacific Coast.

Before leaving Paris, she had wondered what she would find. She was going back "to visit my native land. It may not mean so much to anybody but it does mean a lot to me . . ." The America she had left "was an America where as Mark Twain said in the first diary he ever kept he got up and washed and went to bed. He was proud that every day nothing happened but that that he did get up every day and that he did wash." She hoped that the cities would not be "really different." "One does not like to feel different and if one does not like to feel different then one hopes that things will not look different. It is all right for them to seem different but not to be different."

She discovered that airplanes were as exciting as automobiles: "I like the peaceful hum and the unequal rocking and the way everything looks from them . . ." She lectured in Wisconsin, Minnesota, Michigan, Indiana, Illinois, Missouri, Texas, California. In San Francisco, Gertrude Atherton provided "the smallest oysters there are." In Washington, Mrs. Roosevelt gave her tea. Thornton Wilder lent his apartment in Chicago, where Miss Stein spent several weeks talking to students at the University of Chicago. Carl Van Vechten threw a party in New York. "Everything was a pleasure."

She thought the American roads "were lovely, they move along alone the big ones the way the railroad tracks used to move with really no connection to the country . . . The railroad did not follow the towns made by the road but it made a road followed by the towns in the country, there were no towns and no roads therefore no country until the railroad came along." She found that "there are things like the illustrations of Dante in America there were the walking sleepers in the Chicago marathon and there are the trees in the swamp garden in Charleston." She looked at the big trees in Yosemite that "have no roots did anybody want anything to be more interesting than that that the oldest and the solidest and the biggest tree that could be grown had no foundation . . ." She saw and was excited by a country where "there is more space where nobody is than where anybody is." And that, she concluded, "is what makes America what it is."

The thing that struck me most all over the United States was the physical beauty of the country, and the great beauty of the cities. In Chicago, when I was teaching there, I hired myself a "Drive Yourself" car—I adore the phrase—and drove myself into Chicago every way possible. I don't know a place in the world more beautiful, and I lost my heart to Texas. Then, Toledo was very beautiful, and the way that the city towers rise out of the dead level Northwestern plains was marvelous, and New England under the snow and now in the spring was so lovely.

☆ ☆ ☆

Oklahoma City with its towers that is its skyscrapers coming right up out of the flat oil country was as exciting as when going to Alsace just after the armistice we first saw the Strasbourg Cathedral. They do come up wonderfully out of that flat country and it was exciting and seeing the oil wells and the funny shapes they made the round things as well as the Eiffel Tower ones gave me a feeling like I have in going to Marseilles and seeing the chimneys come out of the earth and there are no houses or anything near them, it always is a strange-looking country that produces that kind of thing, of course Alice Toklas' father had once almost had an oil

49

well they dug and dug but naturally the oil did not gush, naturally not these things never do happen to any one one knows, if it could happen to them you would not be very likely to know them most naturally not. We did later see in California some small oil fields and the slow movement of the oil wells made it perfectly all right that in America the prehistoric beasts moved slowly. America is funny that way everything is quick but really everybody does move slowly, and the movement of the oil well that slow movement very well that slow movement is the country and it makes it prehistoric and large shapes and moving slowly very very slowly so slowly that they do almost stand still. I do think Americans are slow minded, it seems quick but they are slow minded yes they are.

☆ ☆ ☆

What is the United States of America.

It is not a country surrounded by a wall or not as well by an ocean. In short the United States of America is not surrounded.

☆ ☆ ☆

In America they want to make everything something anybody can see by looking. That is very interesting, that is the reason there are no fences in between no walls to hide anything no curtains to cover anything and the cinema that can make anything be anything anybody can see by looking. That is the way it is.

☆ ☆ ☆

I like to think of all these millions of houses each one by itself each one all open each one with the moist food made of good material and each one with the American family inside it really not really afraid of anything in spite of everything in the way of woods and weather and snow and sun and hurricanes and thunder and blizzards any anything.

☆ ☆ ☆

The wooden houses of America excited me as nothing else in America excited me, the skyscrapers and the streets of course and everybody knowing you of course but not like the wooden houses everywhere. I never stopped being excited by the wooden houses everywhere. I liked them all. Almost best I liked those near the railway stations old ones not very old once but still old ones with long flat wooden surfaces, painted sometimes not and many near automobile dumps. I liked them all. I do like a flat surface that is the reason I like pictures and do not like sculpture and I like paint even if it is not painted and wood painted or not painted has the color of paint and it takes paint so much better than plaster. In France and Spain I like barracks because they have so much flat surface but almost I like best American wooden houses and there are so many of them an endless number of them and endless varieties in them. It is what in America is very different, each one has something and well taken care of or neglect helps them, helps them to be themselves each one of them. Nobody could get tired of them and then the windows they put in. That is one thing any American can do he can put windows in a building and wherever they are they are interesting. Windows in a building are the most interesting thing in America. It is hard to remember them because they are so interesting. Every wooden house has windows and the windows are put in in a way that is interesting. Of course the skyscrapers it is a wrong name because in America there is no sky there is air but no sky of course that has a lot to do with why there really is no painting in America no real painting but it is not necessary when there are houses and windows and air. Less and less there are curtains and shutters on the windows bye and bye there are not shutters and no curtains at all and that worried me and I asked everybody about that. But the reason is easy enough. Everybody in America is nice and everybody is honest except those who want to break in. If they want to break in shutters will not stop them so why have them and other people looking in, well as everybody is a public something and anybody can know anything about any one and can know any one then why shut the shutters and the curtains and keep any one from seeing, they all know what they are going to see so why look. I gradually began to realize all this.

☆ ☆ ☆

I have always wanted to write about how one state differs from another. It is so strange that the lines are ruled lines on paper, I never can stop having pleasure in the way the ruled lines separate one state from another. Ohio from Indiana Kansas from Nebraska Tennessee from Alabama, it always gives me a shock of pleasure the American map and its straight lines and compare it to any other with the way they go all over nothing neat and clean like the maps of America. Well that is the way the earth looked to me as we flew to Chicago. They all came and talked to me the pilots and the stewardesses and then I went into the pilot place and talked to them and I sat down in one of their chairs and made the wheel move a little and it was all a pleasant matter but most of all the looking down and finding it a real America. Straight lines and quarter sections, and the mountain lines in Pennsylvania very straight lines, it made it right that I had always been with cubism and everything that followed after.

☆ ☆ ☆

There is nothing that I have ever seen or heard in Europe that has been to me so romantic as when in Oakland California when I was young we went to the railroad station just to get an ordinary local and the man said in a loud voice not to us but to a great many others this way for all points East. It is still for me a romance to be starting for all points East or West or South or North and each one of them a different city and a different state and all of them American.

☆ ☆ ☆

They told us that the modern high buildings had been invented in Chicago and not in New York. That is interesting. It is interesting that it should have been done where there was plenty of land to build on and not in New York where it is narrow and so must be high of necessity. Choice is always more pleasing than anything necessary.

I had no idea that they would throw such a beautiful dark gray light on the city at night but they do. I mean the lights do. The lighting of the buildings in Chicago is very interesting and then I liked the advertisement for dancing that they had at the end of the beginning of everything they had a room and figures dancing solemnly dancing and in the daytime it was the daytime and at night it was nightime and I never tired of seeing them, the sombre gray light on the buildings and the simple solemn mechanical figures dancing, there were other things I liked but I liked that the most.

Chicago may have thought of it first but New York has made it higher much higher. It was the Rockefeller Center building that pleased me the most and they were building the third piece of it when we left New York so quietly so thinly and so rapidly, and when we came back it was already so much higher that it did not take a minute to end it quickly.

It is not delicate it is not slender it is not thin but it is something that does make existence a non-existent real thing. Alice Toklas said it is not the way they go into the air but the way they come out of the ground that is the thing. European buildings sit on the ground but American ones come out of the ground.

☆ ☆ ☆

I liked going over the Salt Lake region the best, it was like going over the bottom of the ocean without any water in it and I was very satisfied with it after all it is nice to know the difference between the ocean with water and the ocean without water in it. After all it is a satisfaction to know that an ocean is interesting even if there is no water in it. That is what I like about America it is interesting even if there is no water in the ocean of it, as some one whom Alice Toklas used to know used to say Lizzie you do know Lizzie what I mean.

But it was what I liked and then the barrier at the end of it and then the ranges the high ranges for the cattle they always tell about that in the stories of the cowboys and then gradually getting down lower, there was not much grass there but then after all America is just as interesting with no water or too much water or no ocean or no grass there that is what I like about America . . .

☆ ☆ ☆

. . . there did not seem to be any inhabitants in Virginia. It was the only place in America where there were no houses no people to see, there were hills and woods and red earth out of which they were made and there were no houses and no people to see. Of course when they fought there it had been called the Wilderness, the campaign in the Wilderness but I had no realization that almost all Virginia was that, after all the novels make it sound inhabited, the stories of it make it sound inhabited but there was of course the days and days of fighting in the Wilderness and I had never thought of that. And then they asked me what I thought of Virginia and I said I thought it was uninhabited, and they all of them wrote about that did I mean spirits of others or did I mean something else and I meant nothing but that it was uninhabited.

The rest of America had been very much inhabited much more than I expected, roads and country were inhabited the country looked and was inhabited but not in Virginia no not Virginia.

☆ ☆ ☆

I did not know that New England had become like Switzerland where there were schools and colleges and hotels and houses. It was that. Everywhere there were schools boys' schools girls' schools and colleges and houses, of course there were some woods and some mountains we went over and through some of them and there was the Atlantic Ocean but otherwise there were schools and colleges and everybody went to school in them. There were hotels too and it was

57

in these hotels men were drunk in them we had not seen men drunk too much anywhere else. We had expected to but we had not. When I was at Radcliffe as a student I naturally knew a great many New England women, naturally I did and of course I read Howells, he is very interesting one can read him again not perhaps as good as Trollope but pretty good and any one can read him again. He too knew that New Englanders had a fear of drinking, they also knew about it in Louisa Alcott I always remembered it in Rose In Bloom and how they worried about offering any one a drink and even about communion wine, any one in that way might suddenly find that they had a taste for drink and I slowly realized that New Englanders might. In California we had all had wine to drink like any Latin and drinking wine can make you drunk but not so very likely. The French with the Americanization of Europe have taken to what in California they used to call hard liquor instead of wine and water. They used to put water in their wine now they drink less quantity but no water in their wine and they drink hard liquor. Well I did realize in New England that that to me mysterious thing they used to talk about a taste for liquor did indeed matter.

☆ ☆ ☆

. . . one of the few things really dirty in America are the drug stores but the people in them sitting up and drinking milk and coffee that part of the drug store was clean that fascinated me. After that I was always going in to buy a detective novel just to watch the people sitting on the stools. It was like a piece of provincial life in a real city. The people sitting on the stools and eating in the drug store all looked and acted as if they lived in a small country town. You could not imagine them ever being out in the streets of New York, nor the drug store itself being in New York. I never had enough of going into them.

☆ ☆ ☆

The ten cent stores did disappoint me but the nut stores not. In the ten cent stores there was nothing that I wanted and what was there was was not there for ten cents. It was a disappointment, I had looked forward to it looked forward to going in and buying at a ten cent store. Alice Toklas says they were not a disappointment but nothing in America was a disappointment to her but they were really they were. But the nut stores I had first known of their existence accidentally from Carl Van Vechten when he happened to say that he one day met Henry McBride as Henry was coming out and Carl was going into a nut store. What is that we had asked excitedly what is a nut store. Then later when he was back in New York he did not forget to send us an ad of a nut store and now here we were and there they were. I was always looking into them.

☆ ☆ ☆

The thing that either has changed or that I have forgotten perhaps it has changed and perhaps I have forgotten, when I come to think about it I do think that I have perhaps forgotten but at any rate it has nothing at all to do with eating are the boxes they put out for the postman on the road the rural delivery. I cannot get used to them, they are such a strange decoration as they sit there on the road side resting on nothing which is a stick to support them.

These boxes are never closed they are always open practically any of them are open and it seems so trusting. Is there no neighbor to wonder or a total stranger to wonder who is doing the letter writing to whom and then to find out about it by looking. It seems so trusting to have all these letter boxes standing there by themselves perilously supported on a stick sometimes one all alone and sometimes a group of them and all of them so that anybody might take them away and everybody could see inside and see that they were open and what is inside of any letter in any one of them. All these things are so trusting and that makes the fascination of the American character, it has so much suspicion in it

of anything and everything and it is so trusting, which is
really very exciting of it to be.

☆ ☆ ☆

We went out on the street and then we went up the
avenues and then down them, and it was wonderful.
Strangeness always goes off very quickly, that is one of
the troubles with traveling but then the pleasure of looking if you like to look is always a pleasure. Alice Toklas
began to complain she said why do they call Paris la
ville lumière, she always prefers that anything should be
American, I said because when they did there were more
lights there than anywhere, you cannot blame them that
they still think so although there are more lights here than
anywhere. And there were. And more beautifully strung
as lights than anywhere except in Spain, and we were
walking along and talking and all of a sudden I noticed
that Alice Toklas was looking queer and I said what is
it and she said my knees are shaking and I said what is it
and she said I just happened to see it, the side of the
building. She just had happened to see it, and if you do
just happen to see one of those buildings well her knees
had not shaken not since the first bomb in 1915 had
fallen in Paris so the sky-scrapers are something.

WE AND THEY

. . . .

"America is my country
and Paris is my home town . . .
I am an American
and I have lived half my life in Paris,
not the half that made me
but the half in which I made what I made."

Miss Stein never spoke of having faith in America; she simply couldn't be without America, and she wanted it to go on being the way it was. It would not be Europe, how could it be. "America's funny," she wrote, "it always thinks it wants what Europe can't have and then it always likes to come and look at what Europe does have, well as my grandfather used to remark there is a great deal to be said on both sides." She took both sides, believing that your parent's home is a nice place to be brought up in, but not to work in.

In Paris, there were pictures, talks, walks through the streets with Basket, the large white poodle who so delighted French children. And there were the long quiet hours in the night when Miss Stein wrote.

France was "the background of all who were excited and determined and created by the twentieth century." But that appreciation did not make her French. When Alice Toklas first came to the rue de Fleurus she "did not realize then how completely and entirely American was Gertrude Stein." Later, Miss Toklas teased her, "calling her a general, a civil war general of either or both sides."

When the first World War broke out, Miss Stein and her companion were in England, staying with the Alfred Whiteheads. The thought of Paris in danger was agony. They could barely listen to news of the German advance, and when Miss Toklas brought word of the German withdrawal, calling out, "it is all right, Paris is safe, the Germans are in retreat," Gertrude Stein turned away and said, "don't tell me these things." "But it's true," Miss Toklas said, "it is true. And then we wept together."

She cherished Paris, she lived there for most of forty-three years. But when she came back to the United States for her lecture tour, and people asked whether she did not find her own country strange, the question meant nothing to her. "After all, I am American all right." Being back home did not make her "more there."

The Renaissance needed the greeks, as the modern painter needed the Negroes as the English writers have needed Italy and as many Americans have needed Spain or France. There is no possibility of mixing up the other civilization with yourself you are you and if you are you in your own civilization you are apt to mix yourself up too much with your civilization but when it is another civilization a complete other a romantic other another that stays there where it is you in it have freedom inside yourself which if you are to do what is inside yourself and nothing else is a very useful thing to have happen to you and so America is my country and Paris is my home town.

After all everybody, that is, everybody who writes is interested in living inside themselves in order to tell what is inside themselves. That is why writers have to have two countries, the one where they belong and the one in which they live really. The second one is romantic, it is separate from themselves, it is not real but it is really there.

The English Victorians were like that about Italy, the early nineteenth century Americans were like that about

Spain, the middle nineteenth century Americans were like that about England, my generation the end of the nineteenth century American generation was like that about France.

Of course sometimes people discover their own country as if it were the other, a recent instance of that is Louis Bromfield discovering America, there have been a few English like that too, Kipling for instance discovered England but in general that other country that you need to be free in is the other country not the country where you really belong.

☆ ☆ ☆

. . . the French newspaper the Intransigeant asked me to write and tell them why I like to live in France. Well the reason is very simple their life belongs to them so your life can belong to you . . .

☆ ☆ ☆

The United States is just now the oldest country in the world, there always is an oldest country and she is it, she who is the mother of the twentieth century civilization. She began to feel herself as it just after the Civil War.

And so it is a country the right age to have been born in and the wrong age to live in.

She is the mother of modern civilization and one wants to have been born in the country that has attained and live in the countries that are attaining or going to be attaining. This is perfectly natural if you only look at facts as they are. America is now early Victorian, very early Victorian, very early Victorian, she is a rich and well nourished home but not a place to work. Your parents' home is never a place to work it is a nice place to be brought up in. Later on there will be place enough to get away from home in the United States, it is beginning, then there will be creators who live at home. A country this the oldest and therefore the most important country in the world quite naturally produces the creators, and so naturally it is I an American who was and is thinking in writing was born in America and lives in Paris. This has been and probably will be the history of the world. That it is always going to be like that makes the monotony and variety of life that and that we are after all all of ourselves.

☆☆☆

There is no thanks or welcome no not in an American religion.

There is no sky, no there is no sky. And why. For the

very simple reason that there is no sky, not in America not in American religion and why. Why is there no sky.

And so you see why American religion and European religion have nothing in common. Nothing at all.

European religion has a sky.

So heaven is there on high.

American religion has no sky and why. Because America has no sky. And why. Because that is why. There is only air and no sky. That is why.

☆ ☆ ☆

. . . there are two things about football that anybody can like. They live by numbers, numbers are everything to them and their preparation is like any savage dancing, they do what red Indians do when they are dancing and their movement is angular like the red Indians move. When they lean over and when they are on their hands and feet and when they are squatting they are like an Indian dance. The Russians squat and jump too but it looks different, art is inevitable everybody is as their air and land is everybody is as their food and weather is and the Americans and the red Indians had the same so how could they not be the same how could they not, the country is large but somehow it is the same if it were not somehow the same it would not remain our country and that would be a shame. I like it as it is.

I remember years and years ago Sayen was a painter in Paris and I used to say to Sayen of course all this was long before there was a war and Americans in Europe in any army and I used to ask Sayen when Americans stand or sit at the Cafe de la Paix not doing anything and then they go away what are they doing what are they thinking what are they saying. He always said nothing. But said I being accustomed to Europeans that is not possible. Yes it is he said well then I said why do they not stay on forever. Oh he said because one of them says I am going, and I said why did he say it then, for no reason said Sayen.

☆ ☆ ☆

I was just listening to an account by one of the American generals of the simple things for which Americans are fighting and the first thing they mention is that you can be in your home and nobody can force their way in and authoritatively frighten you and do whatever they will, I think it is very extraordinary that an American general can so simply understand that that is the horrible thing about an occupied country, the uneasiness in the eyes of all young men and in the eyes of their fathers mothers sisters and brothers, and wives, that uneasiness because at any moment they can be taken away at any moment, their papers can be in order and yet, and then papers can not be in order and also, and just now our neighbors were telling us of a young man we had known him very well in Belley and later here, and he would go out to the nearest town to buy bread, and his mother said no do not, and he said but mother my papers are in order and he went and he did not come back, he was sent, his mother does not know where and his papers were in order and yet, and it is extraordinary that the American general should understand that that is what any American could fight for, that nowhere in the world should those who have not committed any crime should not live peacefully in their home, go peacefully about their business and not be afraid, not have uneasiness in their eyes, not. I do think it very extraordinary that the American general should have so simply understood that.

☆ ☆ ☆

Spaniards and Americans are not like Europeans, they are not like Orientals, they have something in common, that is they do not need religion or mysticism not to believe in reality as all the world knows it, not even when they see it. In fact reality for them is not real and that is why there are skyscrapers and American literature and Spanish painting and literature.

☆ ☆ ☆

Americans . . . are like spaniards, they are abstract and cruel. They are not brutal they are cruel. They have no close contact with the earth such as most europeans have. Their materialism is not the materialism of existence, of possession, it is the materialism of action and abstraction.

☆ ☆ ☆

Gertrude Stein used to get furious when the english all talked about german organisation. She used to insist that the germans had no organisation. Don't you understand the difference, she used to say angrily, any two americans, any twenty americans, any millions of americans can organise themselves to do something but germans cannot organise themselves to do anything, they can formulate a method and this method can be put upon them but that isn't organisation. The germans, she used to insist, are not modern, they are a backward people who have made a method of what we conceive as organisation, can't you see. They cannot therefore possibly win this war because they are not modern.

Then another thing that used to annoy us dreadfully was the english statement that the germans in America would turn America against the allies. Don't be silly, Gertrude Stein used to say to any and all of them, if you do not realise that the fundamental sympathy in America is with France and England and could never be with a mediaeval country like Germany, you cannot understand America. We are republican, she used to say with energy, profoundly intensely and completely a republic and a republic can have everything in common with France and a great deal in common with England but whatever its form of government nothing in common with Germany. How often I have heard her then and since explain that americans are republicans living in a republic which is so much a republic that it could never be anything else.

SUCCESS

. . . .

". . . I am certain that what makes American success
is American failure."

Does success spoil the successful? Not necessarily, Miss Stein thought. She herself "wanted to be historical, from almost a baby on." She wanted to be "a lion, I'd like it again and again, and it is a peaceful thing to be one succeeding." And so when Henry McBride told her that success was the ruination of an artist, she replied that she would "like to have a little, you know. Think of my unpublished manuscripts." Henry McBride was firm: "The best thing that I can wish you is to have no success. It is the only good thing." Then came the Autobiography of Alice B. Toklas and for the first time Miss Stein made money. That was followed by the American tour, she was suddenly a celebrity. She had wanted to appear in the Saturday Evening Post and in the Atlantic Monthly. Both published her articles. Although, like Henry McBride, she "used to tell all the men who were being successful young how bad this was for them," she, "who was no longer young was having it happen."

Well, success or failure had nothing to do with money or with public recognition, or with their absence. Success as a result was exciting, success as an ambition was defeating. Miss Stein thought that a writer fails when the audience takes charge, when a writer composes with the reader looking over his shoulder. She wrote about this kind of failure long before the vogue of books about "outer directed" or "conformist." When she called Ernest Hemingway "ninety percent Rotarian," it was because she thought he was the captive of the readers he wanted. "What a story that of the real Hem," she said,

76

"and one he should tell himself but alas he never will, after all, as he himself once murmured, there is the career, the career."

When she came back to Oakland, California, she was pleased to find that "the papers . . . are full of the Oakland girl who had made good, in a big way," but she had not made good because she had tried to please the Oakland papers. In Hollywood, when they asked her how she had been able to get so much publicity she said, "by having a small audience. I said if you have a big audience you have no publicity . . . they wanted the publicity and the big audience, and really to have the biggest publicity you have to have a small one, yes all right the biggest publicity comes from the realest poetry and the realest poetry has a small audience not a big one, but it is really exciting and therefore has the biggest publicity, all right that is it."

She found, paradoxically, that "most of the great men in America had a long life of early failure and a long life of later failure." Of course they were not failures, they were their own men. And when, toward the end of the second World War, she talked with the G.I.'s in France, she wondered if they would be their own men, whether they would choose to suit themselves. "If the outside puts a value on you and all your inside gets to be outside," yes, you may be a success, but in a way you are a failure.

☆ ☆ ☆

Success is not doing something, success is earning a living, and no good American can earn a living, he can make money but he cannot earn a living, not at all, not he, not he or as well she.

That is what I like. They say that an American can succeed but not at all not he. He can make money but not a living, not at all not he.

☆ ☆ ☆

Americans when they are twenty-one are always organizers I suppose those that really organize later do not organize then, they use up their organizing energy and then well then then they become a failure . . .

☆ ☆ ☆

We went to William and Mary and it was there that I began to talk to them talk to them about everything. I told them what was the use of their being young if they had the same opinions as all of them who were eighty and a hundred then what was the use. Somebody has to have an individual feeling and it might be a Californian or a Virginian. It was a Californian, I can call myself a Californian because I was there from six to seventeen and a Virginian might have an individual feeling, California and Virginia have at one time had a feeling that they were not part just being American, when Alice Toklas a Californian and Pat Bruce a Virginian used to talk about what was American I always said that Richmond and San Francisco did not make anybody know what was American, it was just Virginia and California and is California that now no not now and Virginia well I told them that there was no use in being young if they had the same way of thinking as if they had the opinions and they did have them and the same point of view and they did have them of what Virginia had been. What was the use. And that is all there is about it, it looks as if it might commence and it never does begin and like General Lee they lead themselves to a predestined defeat and knowing it, if they did not know it then it would be a forlorn hope but they know it and so what is the use of their being young, there is none.

☆ ☆ ☆

We talked about and that has always been a puzzle to me why American men think that success is everything when they know that eighty percent of them are not going to succeed more than to just keep going and why if they are not why they do not keep on being interested in the things that interested them when they were college men and why American men different from English men do not get more interesting as they get older. We talked about that a lot at Wesleyan.

☆ ☆ ☆

I said to the Choate teachers I wonder if the boys can ever come to be themselves because you are all so reasonable and so sweet to them that inevitably they are convinced too soon. Is not that the trouble with American education that if they are to be convinced at all they are convinced too soon is it not the trouble with any republican education.

☆ ☆ ☆

Perhaps America since the depression will never be so young again. I suppose it has to happen it does to any dog that he can never be so young again. But then after they get old they do get young again and so this can happen. It is almost happening in Europe but then America is not old enough yet to get young again. They believed the depression was a depression, before that booms had busted a busted boom is not a depression. I know I was so surprised when a banker cousin of mine said he could not believe really believe that the depression was a depression although he did believe it and that worried him. When a boom busted everybody knew it, they used to say who is holding the dollar this week, but now for the first time they were taking the dollar seriously. Well.

I used to worry about that just before the war. I began to worry that employees in America were getting to feel themselves employed and not potential employers, I used to worry because Americans no longer were feeling themselves potentially rich they were still talking that way but they were not feeling that way and yet it was not a settled thing as it is here in France.

☆ ☆ ☆

Too many Americans are dependent for everything on a 'job.' They don't really own anything, and if the job goes, everything is gone . . . an industrial nation is poor, because its people don't own anything. Americans don't own their high standard of living, they only rent it, which means that they are likely to lose it suddenly as so many did in the Depression.

☆ ☆ ☆

The trouble is, Americans aren't land-crazy any more.
That's what the pioneers were, land-crazy, and that's
what all Frenchmen are and always have been, because
they know that owning a place of your own is what gives
you independence and lets you stand on your own feet,
and no body is rich unless he owns his own soil.

☆ ☆ ☆

. . . honest to God Brewsie, can you be a job chaser
and live at the same time, honest to God Brewsie tell
me that can you live and be a job chaser at the same
time, honest to God, Brewsie tell me it, honest to
God Brewsie, honest to God. Honest to God Willie, said
Brewsie.

☆ ☆ ☆

Well, said Brewsie, I begin to know one thing, if industrialism makes a country poor and makes the people of
that country poor because they all have employee minds,
that is job minds, we got to get on top of industrialism
and not have it on top of us. How come, said Jo. Well,

said Brewsie, it sounds harder than it is. How do you get on top of anything that is on top of you, first you got to break it off you, said Jo.

☆ ☆ ☆

. . . oh Willie, I get so worried, I know it is just the most dangerous moment in our history, in a kind of a way as dangerous more dangerous than the Civil War, well they didn't all think alike then, they had lots of complications, and they did think, think how they orated, they did think, and then, said Brewsie, the Civil War was over, and everybody stopped thinking and they began to articulate, and instead of that they became job-hunters, and they felt different all the time they were feeling different, but they were beginning to articulate alike, I guess job men just have to articulate alike, they got to articulate yes or no to their bosses, and yes or no to their unions, they got to articulate alike, and when you begin to articulate alike, you got to drop thinking out, just got to drop it out, you can go on feeling different but you got to articulate the same Gallup poll, yes you do, and it aint no use making it a second ballot, because nobody can think, how can you think when you feel different, you gotta feel different, anybody does have to feel different, but how can you think when you got to articulate alike. Listen to me Willie, listen to me, it's just like that Willie it just is, said Brewsie. I know, said Willie, it's all right, Brewsie, you got it right it's just the way we are, it's just the way it is, but what are you going to do about it Brewsie. Well that's just it, I kind of think, well I kind of feel that our generation, the generation that saw the depression, the generation that saw the war. I did more than see the depression Brewsie, and I did more than see the war, don't you make no mistake about that Brewsie, I did more than see the depression and I did more than see the war. I know Willie, said Brewsie, I know, I know Willie, and there it is, there was the depression and there was the war, yes but back of that, there is job-mindedness, and what can we do about it. No use saying communism communism, it's stimulating to Russians, because they discovered it, but it wouldnt stimulate us any not any at all. No, said Willie, it certainly would not stimulate me. No I know Willie, said Brewsie, no I just know just how it wouldnt stimulate you but Willie, what we gonna do, we got to think, and how can we think when we got to jump from feeling different to articulating the same, and if we could think Willie what could we think. But, said Willie, Brewsie you just got to hold out some hope, you just got to hold it out. That's very easy to say, said Brewsie, but how can you hold out hope, until you got hope and how can you get hope unless you can think and how can you think when you got to go right from feeling inside you kind of queer and worried and kind of scared and knowing something ought to be done about it articulating all the same thing every minute they ask you something and every minute you open your mouth even when nobody has asked you anything. They talk about cognac, they talk about wine and women, and even that they say just exactly alike, you know it Willie, you know it. Sure I know it Brewsie, sure I know it, but just all the same Brewsie you got to hold out some kind of hope you just got to Brewsie. Well, Willie, I have got some kind of hope not really got it, but it's kind of there and that is because all of us, yes all of us, yes we kind of learned something from suffering, we learned to feel and to feel different and even when it comes to think well we aint learned to think but we kind of learned that if we could think we might think and perhaps if we did not articulate all alike perhaps something might happen. But, said Willie, how about all that job-mindedness, Brewsie, yes, said Willie, how can you not be job-minded when you all have to look for jobs and either get a job or not get a job but you have to do all the time with jobs, how can you be not job-minded if you don't do anything but breathe in a job, think Brewsie, answer me that, said Willie.

☆ ☆ ☆

I was always patriotic, I was always in my way a Civil War veteran, but in between, there were other things, but now there are no other things. And I am sure that this particular moment in our history is more important than anything since the Civil War. We are there where we have to have to fight a spiritual pioneer fight or we will go poor as England and other industrial countries have gone poor, and don't think that communism or socialism will save you, you just have to find a new way, you have to find out how you can go ahead without running away with yourselves, you have to learn to produce without exhausting your country's wealth, you have to learn to be individual and not just mass job workers, you have to get courage enough to know what you feel and not just all be yes or no men, but you have to really learn to express complication, go easy and if you can't go easy go as easy as you can. Remember the depression, don't be afraid to look it in the face and find out the reason why, don't be afraid of the reason why, if you don't find out the reason why you'll go poor and my God how I would hate to have my native land go poor. Find out the reason why, look facts in the face, not just what they all say, the leaders, but every darn one of you so that a government by the people for the people shall not perish from the face of the earth, it wont, somebody else will do it if we lie down on the job, but of all things dont stop, find out the reason why of the depression, find it out each and every one of you and then look the facts in the face. We are Americans.

We love sweets like babies, we don't love no lumps of cheese, and tough bread, no we just like to eat soft stuff, soft bread, soft ice-cream, soft chocolate, soft mush, soft potatoes, soft jam, and peanut butter, we don't except at a little meat we dont really chew. Well and if we don't, said Jo. Soft eats make soft men, said Peter. We soft, are we, said Willie. Well aint we, said Peter. Well perhaps we are, said Willie. How soft, said Jo. Too soft, said Ed.

I have been asked are the young men of this war after the war is over, are they going to be sad young men. No I do not think so. And I do not think so for a most excellent reason, they are sad young men already, if you are sad young men then there is a fair chance that life will begin at 30 instead of ending at 30 and I think more or less that is what is going to happen to this generation. . . . God bless them, innocence and a kind heart, yes they will go on, innocence and a kind heart, it worries them, they are troubled, so am I, life will begin at 30 for them, so really did mine, I like them, they like me, we are American. Bless them.

LANGUAGE

· ·

"The American thing is the vitality of movement,
so that there need be nothing against which
the movement shows as movement."

When a student at the University of Chicago asked Gertrude Stein for an explanation of her line, "rose is a rose is a rose," she said: "Now listen! Can't you see that when the language was new—as it was with Chaucer and Homer—the poet could use the name of a thing and the thing was really there? He could say 'o moon' 'o sea' 'o love' and the moon and the sea and love were really there. And can't you see that after hundreds of years have gone by and thousands of poems have been written he could call on those words and find that they were just worn out literary words? The excitingness of pure being had withdrawn from them; they were just rather stale literary words. Now the poet has to work in the excitingness of pure being; he has to get back that intensity into the language. We all know that it's hard to write poetry in a late age; and we know that you have to put some strangeness, something unexpected, into the structure of the sentence in order to bring back vitality to the noun. Now it's not enough to be bizarre; the strangeness in the sentence structure has got to come from a poetic gift, too. That's why it's doubly hard to be a poet in a late age. Now you have all seen hundreds of poems about roses and you know in your bones that the rose is not there. All those songs sopranos sing as encores about 'I have a garden, oh what a garden!' now I don't want to put too much emphasis on that line, because it's just one line of a longer poem. But I noticed that you all know it; you make fun of it, but you know it. Now listen! I'm no fool. I know that in daily life we don't go around saying 'is a . . . is . . . is . . .' yes, I'm no fool; but I think that in that line the rose is red for the first time in English poetry for a hundred years."

She liked "anything that a word can do," but she had no interest in foreign or made-up words. Language should move, "not moving in relation to anything, not moving in relationship to itself but just moving." And she "didn't want, when I used one word, to make it carry with it too many associations. I wanted as far as possible to make it exact, as exact as mathematics; that is to say, for example, if one and one makes two, I wanted to get words to have as much exactness as that."

She often tried to explain to the French what American writing had to be. She used to tell them that at the time she left America the Flatiron Building was "the tallest one and now it is not one at all it is just a house like any house but at that time it was the tallest one and I said you see you look up and you see the cornice up there way on top clear in the air, but now in the new ones there is no cornice up there and that is right because why end anything, well anyway I always explained everything in America by this thing, the lack of passion that they call repression and gangsters, and savagery, and everybody being nice, and everybody not thinking because they had to drink and keep moving, in Europe when they drink they sit still but not in America no not in America and that is because there is no sky, there is no lid on top of them and so they move around or stand still and do not say anything. That makes that American language that

91

says everything in two words and mostly in words of one syllable two words of one syllable and that makes all the conversation. That is the reason they like long books novels and things of a thousand pages it is to calm themselves from the need of two words and those words of one syllable that say everything."

☆ ☆ ☆

. . . the United States had the first instance of what I call Twentieth Century writing. You see it first in Walt Whitman. He was the beginning of movement. He didn't see it very clearly but there was a sense of movement that the European was much influenced by because, the Twentieth Century has become the American Century.

☆ ☆ ☆

. . . here in America because the language was made so late in the day that is at a time when everybody began to read and write all the time and to read what was written all the time it was impossible that the language would be made as languages used to be made to say what the nation which was coming to be was going to say.

☆ ☆ ☆

Bernard Fay was away he was in Sweden and he had an American secretary whose name is Hub and Hub was to meet him in the car and bring him back. Hub had been to dinner with us before leaving and I went out walking in the evening and we walked together down the Boulevard Raspail. And so you are to be back Saturday evening I said as Bernard is to lecture. Are we said Hub. Well of course they did not get back Bernard Fay had remembered to forget but I was there and they asked me would I do it for him.

But that is not what did matter I did but the thing that I remember is that Hub Murphy said are we.

I begin to think then and later more and more that Americans can and do express everything oh yes everything in words of one syllable made up of two letters or three and at most four.

And in some fashion the letters chosen that make up the words of one syllable although they are so few are like letters which would make up a longer word. Are we for example.

☆ ☆ ☆

Then at the same time is the question of time. The assembling of a thing to make a whole thing and each one of these whole things is one of a series, but beside this there is the important thing and the very American thing that everybody knows who is an American just how many seconds minutes or hours it is going to take to do a whole thing. It is singularly a sense for combination within a conception of the existence of a given space of time that makes the American thing the American thing, and the sense of this space of time must be within the whole thing as well as in the completed whole thing.

I felt this thing, I am an American and I felt this thing, and I made a continuous effort to create this thing in every paragraph that I made in The Making of Americans. And that is why after all this book is an American book an essentially American book, because this thing is an essentially American thing this sense of a space of time and what is to be done within this space of time not in any way excepting in the way that it is inevitable that there is this space of time and anybody who is an American feels what is inside this space of time so well they do what they do within this space of time, and so ultimately it is a thing contained within. I wonder if I at all convey to you what I mean by this thing. I will try to tell it in every way I can as I have in all the writings that I have ever done. I am always trying to tell this thing that a space of time is a natural thing for an American to always have inside of them as something in which they are continuously moving. Think of anything, of cowboys, of movies, or detective stories, of anybody who goes anywhere or stays at home and is an American and you will realize that it is something strictly American to conceive a space that is filled with moving, a space of time that is filled always filled with moving and my first real effort to express this thing which is an American thing began in writing The Making of Americans.

☆ ☆ ☆

I was much taken with what one American soldier said when he was in England. He said we did not get along at all with the English until they finally did get it into their heads that we were not cousins, but foreigners, once they really got that, there was no more trouble.

The trouble of course is or was that by the time America became itself everybody or very nearly everybody could read and write and so the language which would naturally have changed as Latin languages changed to suit each country, French, Italian and Spanish, Saxon countries England and Germany, Slav countries etcetera, America as everybody knew how to read and write the language instead of changing as it did in countries where nobody knew how to read and write while the language was being formed, the American language instead of changing remained English, long after the Americans in their nature their habits their feelings their pleasures and their pains had nothing to do with England.

So the only way the Americans could change their language was by choosing words which they liked better than other words, by putting words next to each other in a different way than the English way, by shoving the language around until at last now the job is done, we use the same words as the English do but the words say an entirely different thing.

Yes in that sense Americans have changed, I think of the Americans of the last war, they had their language but they were not yet in possession of it, and the children of the depression as that generation called itself it was beginning to possess its language but it was still struggling but now the job is done, the G.I. Joes have this language that is theirs, they do not have to worry about it, they dominate their language and in dominating their language which is now all theirs they have ceased to be adolescents and have become men.

☆ ☆ ☆

The English from Chaucer to the Elizabethans played with words they endlessly played with words because it was such an exciting thing to have them there words that had come to be the words they had just come to use then.

But the American has a different feeling, these words the words that the Englishman had settled into having as a steady and unchangeable something, they the Americans did not care for the particular use these later Englishmen had come to have for them and the American had then decided that any word which was a word which was there if you put enough pressure upon them if you arranged and concentrated and took away all excrescences from them you could make these same words do what you needed to do with them.

And they did this thing and they are doing this thing and punctuation and arranging them and destroying any connection between them between the words that would that did when the English used them make of them having a beginning and a middle and an ending to them has made of these English words words that move as the Americans move with them move always move and in every and in any direction. It is a very interesting thing that this has been done by the pressure brought to bear upon them brought to bear upon these words which came to us as they were and as they still are but now they have an entirely different movement in them.

Anybody can tell this the minute they pick up any ordinary book any ordinary newspaper any ordinary advertisement or read any ordinary road sign or slang or conversation. The words used are the same words but they have such a different pressure put upon them that in the case of the English the words have the feeling of containing that in which they are staying and with the American they have the feeling that they are and indicate and feel moving existing inside in them.

Notes on Sources

WORKS OF GERTRUDE STEIN QUOTED

"A Patriotic Leading," *Useful Knowledge*,
John Lane, The Bodley Head, Ltd., London, 1928, pp. 81–82

SOLDIERS: THE DOUGHBOYS

Page 19   *Wars I have Seen*, Random House, Inc., New York, 1945,
p. 248
20   *The Autobiography of Alice B. Toklas*, Harcourt Brace and
Company, New York, 1933, p. 230
21   *Wars I Have Seen*, p. 40
21   *The Autobiography of Alice B. Toklas*, pp. 224–227
25   *The Autobiography of Alice B. Toklas*, p. 230
25   *The Autobiography of Alice B. Toklas*, p. 221
26   *The Autobiography of Alice B. Toklas*, pp. 294–295

SOLDIERS: THE G.I.'S

29   *Wars I Have Seen*, p. 247
31   *Wars I Have Seen*, pp. 240–241
32   *Wars I Have Seen*, pp. 244–246
35   *Wars I Have Seen*, pp. 251–254
40   *Brewsie and Willie*, Random House, Inc., New York, 1946,
p. 27
40   *Wars I Have Seen*, p. 248
42   "Off We All Went to See Germany," *Life*, August 6, 1945,
pp. 54–58

LANDSCAPE

45   *What Are Masterpieces*, The Conference Press, Los Angeles,
1940, p. 62
49   Interview, "Gertrude Stein Adores U.S. But Not California,"
The New York Herald Tribune, April 30, 1935
49   *Everybody's Autobiography*, Random House, Inc., New York,
1937, pp. 102–103

Page 50   *Four in America*, Yale University Press, New Haven, Connecticut, 1947, p. 169
50   *Everybody's Autobiography*, p. 196
51   "American Food and American Houses," *The New York Herald Tribune*, April 13, 1935, p. 13
51   *Everybody's Autobiography*, pp. 182–183
53   *Everybody's Autobiography*, pp. 190–191
54   "American Cities and How They Differ from Each Other," *The New York Herald Tribune*, April 6, 1935, p. 13
54   *Everybody's Autobiography*, pp. 201–202
56   *Everybody's Autobiography*, pp. 294–295
56   *Everybody's Autobiography*, pp. 244–245
57   *Everybody's Autobiography*, p. 237
58   *Everybody's Autobiography*, p. 188
59   *Everybody's Autobiography*, p. 187
60   "American Food and American Houses"
61   *Everybody's Autobiography*, pp. 174–175

WE AND THEY

63   *What Are Masterpieces*, pp. 61–62
66   *What Are Masterpieces*, pp. 62–63
66   *Paris France*, Charles Scribner's Sons, New York, 1940, pp. 2–3
67   *Everybody's Autobiography*, pp. 102–103
67   "Why Do Americans Live In Europe?", *Transition*, No. 28, Fall, 1928, p. 97
68   *Four in America*, p. 30
69   *Everybody's Autobiography*, pp. 197–198
70   *Everybody's Autobiography*, p. 109
70   *Wars I Have Seen*, pp. 156–157
71   *Picasso*, Beacon Press, Boston, 1959, p. 18 (by arrangement with B. T. Batsford, Ltd.)
72   *The Autobiography of Alice B. Toklas*, p.111
72   *The Autobiography of Alice B. Toklas*, pp. 187-188

SUCCESS

75   *Lectures in America*, Random House, Inc., New York, 1935, p. 172
78   *Four in America*, p. 16
78   *Everybody's Autobiography*, p. 255
78   *Everybody's Autobiography*, p. 249
79   *Everybody's Autobiography*, p. 239
80   *Everybody's Autobiography*, p. 241
80   *Everybody's Autobiography*, p. 105
81   Continental Edition, *Yank—The Army Weekly*, Nov. 11, 1945

Page 82   Continental Edition, *Yank—The Army Weekly*, Nov. 11, 1945
82   *Brewsie and Willie*, pp. 108–109
82   *Brewsie and Willie*, p. 70
83   *Brewsie and Willie*, pp. 102–106
85   *Brewsie and Willie*, pp. 113–114
87   *Brewsie and Willie*, p. 78
87   "The New Hope in Our 'Sad Young Men,'" *The New York Times Magazine*, June 3, 1945, p 38

LANGUAGE

89   *Lectures in America*, p. 173
93   "How Writing is Written," *The Choate Literary Magazine*, Vol. XXI, No. 2, February, 1935, Wallingford, Connecticut, p. 5
93   *Narration*, The University of Chicago Press, Chicago, Illinois, 1935, p. 7
93   *Everybody's Autobiography*, pp. 113–114
94   *Lectures in America*, pp. 160–161
96   *Wars I Have Seen*, pp. 258–259
97   *Narration*, pp. 13–14